John James Piatt

Poems of House and Home

John James Piatt

Poems of House and Home

ISBN/EAN: 9783744649391

Printed in Europe, USA, Canada, Australia, Japan

Cover: Foto ©Thomas Meinert / pixelio.de

More available books at **www.hansebooks.com**

POEMS

OF

HOUSE AND HOME.

BY

JOHN JAMES PIATT.

BOSTON:
HOUGHTON, OSGOOD AND COMPANY.
The Riverside Press, Cambridge.
1879.

RIVERSIDE, CAMBRIDGE:
STEREOTYPED AND PRINTED BY
H. O. HOUGHTON AND COMPANY.

*I give this Book with sacred gratitude,
Dear One, to you, so gentle, gracious, good,
Whose high and delicate genius breathes but part
Of your pure spirit, sweet person, tender heart.*

CONTENTS.

HOUSE AND HOME:—
   A Dream of Church-Windows
   Counterparts
   The Dark Street
   Song
   Taking the Night-Train
   Mistress of the Ring
   At Home
   Four Happy Walls
   One of Two
   Home-Bells in the Desert
   The Fisherman's Light-House
   His Dream
   White Frost
   A Song of Content
   The Miner's Betrothal
   The Window-Miracle
   The House's Darling
   Homeward on the Train
   A Winter-Morning Idyl
   The Last Fire
   Foresight of Fate
   The Ring of Fastrada
   To a Child
   Passengers
   Her Dream of Loss
   The Trundle-Bed
   The Outside of the Window

CONTENTS.

	PAGE
Nooning at the Half-Way House	72
Wreck	74
A Scattered Family	76
The Land of Memory	78
Blue Sky	81
Dream-World	83
The Dead House-Fire	85
The Buried Wedding Ring	86
Birthplace	89
The Sight of Angels	92
For a Gravestone	93
The Ghost's Entry	94

OTHER POEMS:—

Clio in the Capitol	99
To the Month of March	103
A Tragedy of Long-Bridge	105
To a Lonely Woodland Spring	109
Home-Longing	110
A Voice in Ohio	111
Brevia	115
I. A Certain Conservative	115
II. The White Liar	115
III. A Statue of Jupiter by Phidias	116
IV. New Life	116
V. After-Wealth	117
VI. A Flower in a Book	117
VII. A Moth	118
VIII. Influence of Books	118
IX. With a Gift	119
X. Holy Word	119
The Dead Star	120
Ode	121
The Poet's Bird	129

POEMS OF HOUSE AND HOME.

A DREAM OF CHURCH-WINDOWS.

REDDENING the woodlands dumb and hoary,
    Bleak with long November winds and rains,
Lo, at sunset breathes a sudden glory —
    Breaks a fire on all the western panes!

Eastward far I see the restless splendor
    Shine through many a window-lattice bright;

Nearer all the farm-house gables render
   Flame for flame, and melt in breathless light.

Many a mansion, many a cottage lowly,
   Lost in radiance, palpitates the same,
At the touch of beauty, strange and holy,
   All transfigured in the evening flame.

Flutters everything with newer being,
   Richer life than ever breathed before;
By the alchemy of clearer seeing,
   Golden lie the shadows — dark no more.

. . . . Far away beyond the Eastern ocean,
   Dreaming in the sunset I behold,
With a restless, palpitating motion,
   Great enchanted windows burn with gold:

High cathedral windows hushed in glory,
   Where the gorgeous priest of Time is Art,
Blazoned miracles of marvelous story,
   Deep in many an olden city's heart.

And I dream that in their inner splendor
   Saints and martyrs shine in ancient fire,
While above, in twilight dusk and tender,
   Angels whiten with divine desire.

All the air is peopled with a vision;
   Seraphs breathe their breath of music there;
Men who made their lives a holy mission
   Show their souls in marble everywhere.

But, within, some stranger's heart is haunted
   With the faiths of homelier altars bright,

Saints in dearer window-glow enchanted,
    Till his face is dark with saddened light.

And he sees in dream the woodlands hoary,
    Bleak with long November winds and rains,
Reddened while the level sunset glory
    Floats on all the western window-panes;

Sees, as I do, while the phantom splendid
    Of those gorgeous windows passes bright,
And the radiance, which my dream attended,
    Slowly fades and falters into night:

While abroad the bare and dumb November
    Ghost-like stands amid the crimson haze,
And the glimmering casements scarce remember,
    Ghost-like in the gloom, the sunset blaze:—

Sees a sudden, newer, dearer splendor
  Issue from a thousand windows warm,
Where the children crowd with faces tender,
  Guarded by the fireside's sacred charm.

Let me leave the twilight's dusk reflection,
  And the ghosts that walk the autumnal night :—
Wife and mother, with divine affection,
  Stand within the western window-light.

COUNTERPARTS.

A LOVER'S CONCEIT.

I SEND, Sweet, my yearning
  Half-kisses to thee;
Oh, send thy returning
  Half-kisses to me.

When our half-kisses meet, love,
  What marvels have birth! —
All fair things, and sweet, love;
  New Heaven, new Earth!

THE DARK STREET.

O WEARY feet that fill the nightly air!
    No hearts I hear, no faces see above;—
I feel your single yearning, everywhere,
    Moving the way of Love!

Forever crowding weary, one by one
    Ye pass no more through all the shadowy air;
The footsteps cease on thresholds dearly lone —
    Quick hearts, glad faces there!

There all the voices of the heart arise,
    Unheard along the darkling street before:
The faces light their loving lips and eyes,
    The footsteps are no more!

SONG.

Give me a home, thy heart,
    For Love to lie in:
The world is wide — oh, let
    The lost dove fly in.

Give me a home, thy heart,
    For Song to light in,
For dreary hours to dream
    And waken bright in.

Give me a home, thy heart,
    For Love to see in,
For Earth to look like Heaven,
    And Heaven to be in!

TAKING THE NIGHT-TRAIN.

A TREMULOUS word, a lingering hand, the burning
  Of restless passion smouldering — so we part;
Ah, slowly from the dark the world is turning
  When midnight stars shine in a heavy heart.

The streets are lighted, and the myriad faces
  Move through the gaslight, and the homesick feet
Pass by me, homeless; sweet and close embraces
  Charm many a household — laughs and kisses sweet.

From great hotels the stranger throng is streaming,
    The hurrying wheels in many a street are loud;
Within the depot, in the gaslight gleaming,
    A glare of faces, stands the waiting crowd.

The whistle screams; the wheels are rumbling slowly,
    The path before us glides into the light:
Behind, the city sinks in silence wholly;
    The panting engine leaps into the night.

I seem to see each street a mystery growing,
    In mist of dreamland — vague, forgotten air:
Does no sweet soul, awakened, feel me going? —
    Loves no dear heart, in dreams, to keep me there?

MISTRESS OF THE RING.

INSCRIBED TO A BRIDE.

AH, little ring of gold!—all one,
    Two lives are in its tender power;
  Two morning paths together flower,
Two hearts beat toward the westering sun.

. . . . On the sweet band was laid a charm:
    Whoe'er its golden orb should wear,
    Her years unblighted May should bear,
With Love to guard her close and warm.

The spell-wrought bond should fold within
    That circle of the enchanter's might

All gentle spirits of joy and light,
The dawn-touched Eden pure of sin.

Clasped in its sacred round should glow
   The gracious atmosphere of Home,
   Whose angels each from Heaven should come,
And, vanishing, to Heaven should go.

Held safe in that enchanted air,
   How fair to her and how serene
   The storm-dark world should still be seen
Beneath the rainbow lighted there!

All fortunes should by her be won:—
   Their myrtle and cypress deathless friends,
   Years, many as Heaven for blessing sends,
Bright as to earth Heaven gives the sun.

This was the precious spell. Behold
   (So may its working follow true)
   I set its charm to words for you —
See on your hand that spell-bound gold!

AT HOME.

FAR off the sunset-smitten spires
   Breathe through the wood their golden fires;
Hither the noisy city swells
A dreamy tide of vesper bells.

FOUR HAPPY WALLS.

PRAYER AT HOUSE-WARMING.

FOUR happy walls to shut the dark away,
  Four happy walls to keep the light secure:
These we call ours — oh, make them yours, we pray,
  Kind gods of the hearth, domestic guardians sure.
Four walls shall close our sphere of love complete,
  Though all the world within our love we fold; —

Oh, bless our threshold, make our hearth your seat :
Our home your heaven, your home our heaven hold !

ONE OF TWO.

LISTEN and look! If you listen, you see
A nest with a bird in yonder tree:
Above, in the leaves that glitter with May,
The little half-owner is singing to-day:
"We are very proud, we are rich, and blessed—
Come and look, if you please, at our nest."

Listen and look! If you look, you hear
The sweetest song you have heard for a year;
Over the nest, on the tremulous spray,
The little half-owner is singing to-day:
"Soon, in the nest I have asked you to see,
Listen and look for our family!"

HOME-BELLS IN THE DESERT.

[FROM AN INCIDENT DESCRIBED IN KINGLAKE'S
"EOTHEN."]

SWEET Sabbath morn! The summer breeze
   With English sunshine fills the trees
  About the church-tower old,
Whose bells o'erflow the vale, and steal
Through green, deep lanes, with gentle peal,
  To many a home's dear fold.

. . . . Through the dead sand, the boundless glare,
The blinding silence everywhere,
  (He veiled from that fierce flame,)

They reach a wanderer's dream : awake,
Those bells the awe-filled silence break, —
   He hears them all the same !

Enchantment ! May a mother's prayer
Have breathed those wondrous travelers there, —
   Far chimes of mother-land ! —
To call her wanderer's worship home ?
Oh, softly clear and near they come
   With Sabbath o'er the sand !

Or may some flying dream have sent
Through Memory's passive instrument
   A breath, those chimes to start,
That, vibrant in the sunshine still,
The desert air with music fill,
   And echo in his heart ?

He knows not, but, dream-like, he sees
That church-tower old, its clustered trees,
　In far familiar air.
'T is Sabbath morn in mother-land :
Those home-bells make, through the hot sand,
　Their gentle visit there!

What blissful vision he perceives!—
Through sunny liftings of the leaves,
　White gleams and faces known :
Dear church-paths old; and one glad door
Opens,—its rose's fragrance o'er
　The desert's breath has blown!

THE FISHERMAN'S LIGHT-HOUSE.

A PICTURE in my mind I keep,
   While all without is shiver of rain;
Warm firelit shapes forgotten creep
   Away, and shadows fill my brain.

I see a chill and desolate bay
   That glimmers into a lonely wood,
Till, darkling more and more away,
   It grows a sightless solitude.

No cheerful sound afar to hear,
   No cheerful sight afar to see;—
The stars are shut in heavens drear,
   The darkness holds the world and me.

Yet hark!—I hear a quickening oar,
    The burden of a happy song,
That echo keeps along the shore
    In faint-repeating chorus long.

And whither moves he through the night,
    The rower of my twilight dream?
A compass in his heart is bright,
    And all his pathway is a gleam!

No light-house leaning from the rock
    To tell the sea-tossed mariner
Where breakers, fiercely gathering, shock—
    A fiery-speaking messenger!

But see, o'er water lighted far,
    One steadfast line of splendor come!—

THE FISHERMAN'S LIGHT-HOUSE.

Is it in heaven the evening-star?
  The fisher knows his light at home!

And which is brighter — that which glows
  His evening star of faith and rest,
Or that which, sudden-kindled, goes
  To meet it from his eager breast?

HIS DREAM.

IN ABSENCE.

WAS it a blissful dream I dreamed,
   Or Fancy's sleepless make-belief?
She came — oh, was she here or seemed? —
   A gentle vision brief;
And, like a rose-tree over me,
She kissed, she clasped me tenderly.

Was it a blissful dream I dreamed,
   Or Fancy's sleepless make-belief?
She came — oh, was she here or seemed? —
   A happy vision brief;

And bent, caressing, and caressed,
A moment's heaven, upon my breast!

It was a blissful dream I dreamed,
   Or Fancy's sleepless make-belief;
She came — she was not here but seemed —
   A flying vision brief.
O soft and vanished dream — despair
Of solitude and empty air!

WHITE FROST.

THE ghostly Frost is come,
  I feel him in the night;
The breathless leaves are numb,
  Motionless with affright:
The moon, arisen late and still,
Sees all their faces beaded chill.

The ghostly Frost is here,
  I see him in the night;
Through all the meadows near
  Waver his garments white:
Ha! at our window, looking through?—
Ah, Frost, this fire would conquer you!

A SONG OF CONTENT.

THE eagle nestles near the sun;
    The dove's low nest for me!—
The eagle's on the crag: sweet One,
    The dove's in our green tree.
For hearts that beat like thine and mine,
    Heaven blesses humble earth;
The angels of our Heaven shall shine
    The angels of our hearth!

THE MINER'S BETROTHAL.[1]

THE miner kissed his maiden bride. "Upon
    St. Lucia's Day,
Their blessing on our lives, fast-bound, the priestly
    palms shall lay;
Then we will build our lucky nest in summer trees
    together,
Where Peace and Love, like singing-birds, shall
    keep their sunny weather."

[1] The story is related of a young miner, somewhere in the north of Europe, whose body was found, fifty years after his death by the falling in of a mine, preserved life-like by some chemical property in the earth, and was recognized only by the faithful woman, grown old and withered, to whom he had been betrothed.

THE MINER'S BETROTHAL.

Yesterday came the Sabbath when, oh, brightly everywhere
The earth was wreathed divinely with the heavenly halo-air;
And in the village chapel, for the second time proclaimed,
The holy bans were spoken, and the happy morrow named.

"Good-morning," at her window now he greets her, going by,
Down to the midnight mine all day — her smile's her bright reply:
"Good-morning," in his heart it sings, and merrily and fast
From her sweet sight he vanished — far away into the Past!

Glad-hearted plays her needle, and her work is
 made of song;
Fancies at loving work for Love lighten slow Time
 along.
Slowly the morning dies and slow the evening
 hours depart,
And in her cheek the roses climb — their fragrance fills her heart.

. . . . Fifty long years of happy Junes and dreary,
 dark Decembers!
Fifty long years of smiles and tears — bright fire-
 sides, dying embers!
Fifty long years — on what strange shores have
 crawled their broken waves! —
How far away their echoes dead drop down in
 Memory's caves!

Old crowns from dust gleam, buried, and old scep-
    tres lie forgot ;
Old prisons, earthquake-shaken low, have opened
    doors for Thought ;
Gray, giant slumberers have awaked with blindness
    in their eyes ;
The West has rounded toward the East more
    manly destinies.[1]

Some miners toil within a mine one morning bright
    and fair,
In olden excavations deep below that morning air :
When lo ! a dreamer lying there, asleep in youth
    benign !
And with his dream about him, fresh, they bring
    him from the mine.

[1] The French and American Revolutions had meanwhile taken place.

No one remembers, seeing him. None know him.
　　Who is he?—
Lying a dreamer all alone, a man of mystery?
Full of the love-dream long ago, he seems a
　　dreamer now:
Yesterday's kiss is in his heart, this morning's on
　　his brow!

They are all gone, they are all gone, the close-
　　familiar faces;
Old footsteps falter far away, old echoes lose their
　　places:
No father, no mother, no brother, steals among
　　that crowd to see
And find his lost face in their hearts, a buried
　　memory.

But who is she that comes, her hands long weary
    with their part? . . . .
From the old coffin of her love he wakens in her
    heart!
Love, only sleeping there like him, leaps up as live
    and young
As when the dews of the far days to Maying
    roses clung.

Her eyes unblinded by the years of patient-wait-
    ing pain,
She claims him for her own, long-lost; she clasps
    him back again:
To a true heart she clasps him back; her wrinkled
    features trace
Life's paths of sorrow fifty years — Death has not
    seen his face!

"Good-morning," long ago he said; he comes to
    say " Good-even."

Love that has lived so long on earth has moulted
    wings for heaven.

A few more days, the appointed time, the bless-
    ing One shall lay;

She knows her fixed betrothal, and she waits the
    wedding-day.

THE WINDOW-MIRACLE.

IT blossomed here on the window,
   All the long, still winter night,
While the Earth in moonshine slumbered
   With face upturned and bright.

It blossomed here on the window,
   The phantom-summer of Frost,
With trees and flowers and foliage —
   All loveliness that is lost.

The children, awakened at dawning,
   Stand gazing with hushed delight;
They see, with sight beyond seeing,
   This miracle of the Night!

THE HOUSE'S DARLING.

O SWEET, shy girl, with roses in her heart
   And love-light in her face, like those upgrown;
Full of still dreams and thoughts that, dreamlike, start
   From fits of solitude when not alone!
Gay dancer over thresholds of bright days,
   Tears quick to her eyes as laughter to her lips!—
A game of hide-and-seek with Time she plays,
   Time hiding his eyes from her in blithe eclipse.

O gentle-souled! — how dear and good she is,
  Blessed by soft dews of happiness and love;
Cradled in tenderest arms! Her mother's kiss
  Seals all her good-night prayers. Her father's smile
Brightens her mornings. Through the Earth shall move
  Her child-sweet soul, not far from Heaven the while!

HOMEWARD ON THE TRAIN.[1]

WHAT homes are waiting now
    With doors ajar, with quickening hearts,
    — the smile
Of firelit quiet touching lip and brow —
    For us, far off the while!

    Tidings have gone before —
Swift messengers, that traverse without fear
Darkness as day, whispering through many a
    door
    Whose threshold knows us near!

[1] On seeing a laden coffin one winter night taken on board a railway train.

For some, perchance, the years
Have traveled with their faces, that to-night
Return — ah, yes, from change, and Time, and
    tears ! —
    Where breathed their morning light.

                •

    And some but yesterday
Kissed parting lips, then smiling dared to
    part,
Trusting to-morrow, with its constant ray,
    Should light heart back to heart.

    . . . . But who is he ? — what door
Is open now for him ? — What mother stands,
Yearning to fold her wanderer safe once more
    From the world's restless sands ?

What faithful one beside
Hope's gentle watch-fire waits for Love's new
bliss ? —
What children, playing in Time's crawling tide,
Hold lips for father's kiss ?

One silent passenger,
In the quick press of eager tongue and brain !
Whither ? I know not, nor who waits him there.
He travels on the train !

Ah me ! if some glad door,
To-morrow, reaches longing arms for him,
Joyous come home ! (He has gone home before.)
There bright eyes must grow dim !

Travelers, near or far !
Remember, loosening hands (ah, clasp again !)
The silent passenger in yonder car,—
Death travels on every train !

A WINTER-MORNING IDYL.

HAUNTING the darkness everywhere,
   The snow has clothed the moonless air
   Through the long hush of night;
And now with morn the woodlands fill
Their solitude, how bright! how still!—
   The valley hides in light!

The sunrise through our window sees
Illumined towers, illumined trees,
   That melt in silver gleams,
Where the weird Artist of the Night,
To give the child a new delight,
   Has tried to paint its dreams!

The trees with dropping sparkles glisten
Beside our door: and — see them! listen! —
    A dozen boys, aglow,
Warm-blooded, full of buoyant life,
Mingle, knee-deep, in merry strife —
    Mock-battles with the snow!

Losing the winter in their joy,
What shouts! what laughter! Yonder boy,
    A champion lithe and tall,
Compels his corps with instant will —
An avalanche charge! But, massed and still,
    These neither fly nor fall!

One little rogue, so cunning-shy,
Powders the large boy in his eye:
    With quick-averted face

Another throws — a cap is flying ; —
To escape the ball another trying
    Slips in soon-lost disgrace!

. . . . Who, smiling, watches, eager, there?
An old man — hoar-frost in his hair,
    But flower-warmth in his heart —.
At yonder window, peering through,
Joins in the happy battle, too,
    His boyhood taking part!

THE LAST FIRE.

[BEFORE LEAVING A FIRST DWELLING-HOUSE.]

THE first fire, one remembered night
    Of chilly Fall, we kindled ; bright
        And beautiful were its gleams !
Warming the New World all our own,
And welcoming radiant futures, shone
        That prophecy of our dreams !

Our window burned against the cold,
And faces from the dark, behold,
        In transient halos came !

The household troubadour of Mirth,
The cricket, took with song our hearth
    And blessed the blessing flame.

O flushing firelight, rosy-warm!
O walls, with many a floating form
    Of dreamy shade a-bloom!
Fancy, by Love transfigured, wrought
All miracles of tender thought,
    Transfiguring the room!

Beloved and blessed and beautified,
God-given Angel at my side!
    The winter came and went;
And never since the world began
Grew sweeter happiness to man,
    Or tenderer content.

THE LAST FIRE.

At dawn we leave the place, so warm
And bright with you, December's storm
    Nor cold nor shadow brought;
The Last Fire clothes our walls to-night —
Our window breathes its wonted light,
    But sadness haunts our thought.

By tenderest tides of feeling stirred,
(Your heart brings tears for every word,)
    I hear you murmur low:
"Here blossomed Home for you and me; —
Love walked without his glamoury,
    And stood diviner so.

"Dear echoes, answering day by day! —
We cannot take the past away!
    The threshold and the door,

Where Love's familiar steps have been
Repeated evermore within,
    Are dear for evermore!"

Yes, but the place beloved shall be
Bequeathed to loving Memory;—
    The spirits of the place,
The Lares of the household air,
Born of the heart, the heart shall bear:
    They know no stranger's face.

The atmosphere we fill is ours;
It moves with us its sun, its showers;
    It is our world alone,
Vivid with all our souls create,
The plastic dream, the stone of Fate.
    We take and keep our own.

So let the Last Fire flame and fall,
The ghostly ember-shadows crawl,
    The ashes fill the hearth :
The cricket travels where we go,
And Home is but the Heaven below,
    Transfiguring the Earth !

FORESIGHT OF FATE.

MOTHER and child walk in a path of flowers,
    Through a bright garden tended by the
Hours.

From gentle blossoms, fragrant-hearted there,
Birds, singing, lift the child's heart into air.

Some dreadful House before them grows, unknown:
A ghostly grated casement stares from stone!

Whence came the phantom?— what enchantment
    wild?
The mother sees it not, nor can the child.

FORESIGHT OF FATE.

Lo, some lost face, haunting with dreamy glare
The darkness, looking through the darkness there!

How strange if he, lost to himself within,
Were that same child, pure as a rose from sin;

And if that face, through those fierce bars aglare,
Saw that same child cling to that mother's care!

THE RING OF FASTRADA.

THE little ring you fondly show
  Is the same ring Fastrada wore,
Wife of the Great Charles long ago —
  Whose charm could bind him evermore.

Living, she held him with its spell;
  Dying, she drew and kept him near;
He clung to her, beloved so well; —
  He would not leave her precious bier.

O dearest, gentlest, sweetest, best!
  Whose eyes of starry tenderness
So many happy years have blest,
  So many more I pray shall bless:

The world-old Magic-Master brought
  You the same ring — if not the same,
The self-same charm in this he wrought
  Which gave to that romantic fame.

Living, you hold me with its spell ;
  Dying, would draw and keep me near,
To cling to you, beloved so well ; —
  How could I leave your precious bier ?

TO A CHILD.

OH, while from me, this tender morn, depart
    Dreams vague and vain and wild,
Sing, happy child, and dance into my heart,
    Where I was once a child!

Your eyes they send the butterflies before,
    Your lips they kiss the rose;
O gentle child, Joy opes your morning door —
    Joy blesses your repose!

The fairy Echo-children love you, try
    To steal your loving voice;
Flying you laugh — they, laughing while you fly,
    Gay with your glee rejoice.

TO A CHILD.

Oh, while from me, this tender morn, depart
    Dreams vague and vain and wild,
Play, happy child, — sing, dance, within my heart,
    Where I will be a child!

PASSENGERS.

NIGHT held aloft the gentle star,
   Her earliest watch-fire in the dark,
And by the window of the car
   Fluttered and flew the hurrying spark.

Its pathway finding through the snows,
   The train rushed on with tremulous roar —
Like one whose purpose burns and glows,
   A torch to lead his life, before.

The darkness grew around the face
   Of every traveler for the night:
A sudden vision filled the place
   And touched the gloom with tender ligh

Not from the holy world unknown: —
   A gentle mission of the air
From happy hearth and threshold flown,
   Familiar angels gathered there.

O prayers that breathe from faces bright,
   O thoughts of love that will not sleep,
O dreams that give the soul by night
   Its wings the body may not keep!

Not unattended, far away,
   The wanderer moves with throngs unknown
Ye meet or follow, night or day —
   I saw your heavenly shapes alone!

HER DREAM OF LOSS.

IN a dark cavern is a frail flower sown,
    The orphan of a beam
In some fair garden of the Sun. Alone,
    In darkness and in dream,

It grows and gropes for the far light above,
    Whose sweet tradition old
Haunts its pure-lifted face. An imaged dove
    Nestling, its wings doth fold

In the blind flower's white core. . . . . My heart I know
    That sunless flower to be.
Oh! dear lost face, Earth's cavern far below
    Prisons my love for thee!

THE TRUNDLE-BED.

Do you remember, Will? — long, long ago!
.... Yet there thou liest, though all the sweet
   Past lies dead,
That nestled in thee, old, old trundle-bed!
Nest of delicious fancies, dreams that grow
No more! — quick magic-car to Fairyland!
   Ghosts walked the earth then (in our garret
      too:
   For Madge, the housemaid, told us — and she
      knew!)
In thee we saw them near, how near us, stand!
Stars then looked out of Heaven; to Heaven,
   light

Prayers clothed like angels from our lips arose,
Though from the heart of her who bent so close,
Hushing us like fixed flowers that feel the night.
. . . . Fresh morn, poor little dreamers lost or dead,
No more shall rouse them from their lowly bed.

THE OUTSIDE OF THE WINDOW.

THEY stand at the window, peering,
   And pressing against the pane
Their beautiful, childish faces:
   Without are the night and rain.

They stand at the window, peering —
   What see they, the children, there?
A room full of happy faces,
   A room full of shining air:

A room full of warmth and brightness,
   A room full of pleasant sights —

Of pictures, and statues, and vases,
   And shadows at play with the lights.

But sweetest of all, to their gazing,
   (So near they seem part of them there!)
Is the room full of happy faces
   In the room full of shining air.

Ah me! my precious observers,
   Another sight I shall find ———
"What is it?" I dread to tell you,
   And, oh, it were sweet to be blind!

From the lighted room, through the window,
   I see, and have seen them of old,
A world full of wretched faces,
   A world full of darkness and cold:

A world full of cold and darkness,
    A world full of dreary sights, —
No pictures, nor statues, nor vases,
    But shadows that put out the lights.

Ah, saddest of all, through the window
    (They seem with us, so near!) I behold
A world full of wretched faces,
    In a world full of darkness and cold!

NOONING AT THE HALF-WAY HOUSE.

A BIRTHDAY.

HERE at the Half-way House, a one-hour's
    guest,
I see far back, in yon bright valley deep,
A tender mother rock her child asleep
In the warm cradle of her happy breast;
And, forward, where the path I go must lead —
Downward how far I cannot guess nor know —
In thick, blind mist, a house secure, but low,
Where I shall rest to-night, and shall not heed
The fierce, sharp tempest on the beaten wold
Nor the close darkness . . . . I will journey on

(Short is the steep descent, the old guides have
 told),
In trust that when the anxious day is gone,
My sleep shall be the same — how soft and
 mild ! —
As, on my mother's breast, yon new-born child.

WRECK.

I.

After the tempest-roar
 The shell sighs on the shore.

A ship shines, rosily,
One sail-gleam, far at sea.

Waves toss, near by, a mast —
The last Hope climbed it last.

II.

After the tempest-roar
The shell sighs on the shore.

A maiden, by the sea,
Sees the sail shine rosily.

On shore the mast is flung —
The dead Hope, dying, clung!

A SCATTERED FAMILY.

WE have been all together on the earth;
    But now the band that bound our gentle sheaf
Is loosed — the powerful magic bond of birth;
Our hearts no longer turn one golden leaf
Each day; no more, through every winter night,
Brightening within though skies without may frown,
We all are gathered close about one light,
With loving wreaths the warm quick hours to crown :
For the one word of "Home," which we had worn,
From the soul's lips, to worldly language clear,

Returns an alien answer to its sound,
From other firesides, winter-lighted, borne. . . . .
"Home!" — 't was a word of Heaven homeless here,
Whose wandering echo in our hearts we found!

THE LAND OF MEMORY.

DEEP in some far enchanted sunshine closed,
  (We sigh and dream but pass forever on,)
Shines a fair Land. The glad young Morning
    there
Comes up as rosily from the lighted East
As over the green walls of Paradise;
There noonday gathers only blissful calm;
There twilight nestles, a still bird of Heaven,
With purple wings o'er soft delicious vales.
Oh, you may know the beauty of that Land
By those that travel hither from its bounds —
Through the cold faces, through the shapes ma-
    lign

That gather round us, through the dreary toils
That bar us like a prison, lo! they come,
By sweet enchantment opening doors of air!

It is no silent Land! — the joyous birds,
That filled lost hours so full with singing, sing
From sunlit bough to bough, shaking the leaves
Among the dancing blossoms of the rain
In sunshine, while the rainbow clings above;
And dear blithe brooks leap on, forever, laugh-
    ing,
Prattling their silver fancies everywhere,
Like children lost whom all things know and love.
Ah, 't is no silent Land, for they are there,
Kind words, there never dead, from voices kind,
That feed the longing of the soul with love.

Transplanted deep in that enchanted earth,
Nothing grows old, leaves fall not, nor flowers
    die;
The plow of change goes over no old graves
In the dear face and in the loving heart.
O loveliest Land in all the sphere of Time! —
Far green oasis girt by restless sand,
Circling with barren sky our empty life,
While with tired limbs and thirsty lips we yearn
For its bright fountains glittering to our eyes,
Only returning to returning dreams! —
O ever-blossoming Land of Memory!

BLUE SKY.

WHEN dreary rains have veiled the day
    For many darkling hours,
Till birds forget their singing May
    And bees their honey-flowers:
How quickens all the earth anew
    If, 'mong the clouds alone,
A single break of happy blue
    By the dark heaven is shown!

"Blue sky! blue sky!" we cheerily cry;
    Our pulses waken new;
Our hearts, uplifted, blithe and high,
    Sing, lark-like, in the blue!

Blue sky! blue sky! An open door,
Though small, may hold the sun,
And through it watchful Hope once more
Sees her Bright Day begun!

DREAM-WORLD.

DEAR, beautiful, far Land!
　　Where all these foot-sore, sighing
　　　　pilgrims go,
Leaving their burden and the restless woe
　　Of the fierce desert sand!

　　Thither all travel : there
Wander tired kings, with glad content, uncrowned ;
The slave, with all his tread-mill bands unbound,
　　Breathes its unguarded air.

　　Thither go home at night
All hopeless exiles in this foreign mart,

Finding the old ways reopened in each heart
    Into forgotten light.

    There the lost child is found : —
O gentle school-boy, vanished from our sight,
Fling your gay ball and fly your eager kite
    In that enchanted ground!

    There, firm as in far years,
Are fallen heart-temples, dear remembered homes;
Through vanished doors each face familiar comes
    Smiling — we wake with tears!

    How far, yet near, it seems!
This dusty world struck underfoot away —
Circling lost suns, and sweet with happier day,
    The holy sphere of dreams!

THE DEAD HOUSE-FIRE.

An hour ago the fireside gleamed
    And merry faces and glances beamed.

Mother and children, with happy sire,
A garland of gladness, wreathed the fire.

There were loving voices and laughing eyes,
Whispers of joy and tender replies.

A ghost in the darkness flutters a flame,
Then drops in the ashes whence it came.

Ghost-like in the gloom the faces grow,
Then fade in my heart with the ember-glow.

THE BURIED WEDDING-RING.

ACROSS the door-step, worn and old,
    The new bride, joyous, passed to-day;
The gray rooms showed an artful gold,
    All words were light, all faces gay.

Ah, many years have lived and died
    Since she the other vanished one,
Into that door, a timid bride,
    Bore from the outer world the sun.

O lily, with the rose's glow!
    O rose, the lily's garment clad!—

The rooms were golden long ago,
  All words were blithe, all faces glad.

She wore upon her hand the ring,
  Whose frail and human bond is gone —
A coffin keeps the jealous thing
  Radiant in shut oblivion :

For she (beloved, who loved so well),
  In the last tremors of her breath,
Whispered of bands impossible —
  " She would not give her ring to Death."

But he, who holds a newer face
  Close to his breast with eager glow,
Has he forgotten her embrace,
  The first shy maiden's, long ago ?

Lo, in a ghostly dream of night,
 A vision, over him she stands,
Her mortal face in heavenlier light,
 With speechless blame but blessing hands!

And, smiling mortal sorrow's pain
 Into immortal peace more deep,
She gives him back her ring again —
 The new bride kisses him from sleep!

BIRTHPLACE.

I PASS it in the dead of night; —
  The autumnal heaven shines misty-bright;
The old moon rises, a dumb ghost
Of the sweet suns whose souls are lost;
The fog crawls o'er the tide asleep,
Like a weird spirit of the deep:
The place whose trees remember me,
Floating in mist, dream-like, I see,
And, mist-like rising, ghostly bright,
Lost memories haunt my soul to-night.

Is it a dream? O Spirit, here
The very dust to thee was dear;

BIRTHPLACE.

The lips of Nature kissed thine own
And blessed thee with her mother-tone,
Giving thee gifts of birds and flowers
And constant miracles of hours:
Oh, in the woods and streams and streets
Perchance the mother-tongue repeats
The dear soft syllables of old —
But thou art deaf, and blind, and cold!

No longer are her arms the birth
Of every precious thing of earth;
No longer on her bosom sweet
Their prayers with thine the flowers repeat.
Is the old Mother blind, that now
She finds no mark on breast or brow? —
Is the dear Mother deaf, she hears
Not her child's voice with mother-ears? —

Is the sweet mother's bosom dry,
She knows not of her nursling nigh?
Alas, the prodigal ne'er returns
For whom the mother's bosom yearns:
Is it not he, the favored one
That was her jewel of the sun
And made it bright. She murmurs, "Come.
My lost one never reaches home."

THE SIGHT OF ANGELS.

THE angels come, the angels go,
   Through open doors of purer air;
Their moving presence oftentimes we know,
   It thrills us everywhere.

Sometimes we see them: lo, at night,
   Our eyes were shut, but open seem;
The darkness breathes a breath of wondrous light,
   And then it was a dream!

FOR A GRAVESTONE.

THE marble has no speech but that we give,
   And we are dumb, and, speechless, pass away;
The silence in which our affections live
   Holds all we need to speak and cannot say.

THE GHOST'S ENTRY.

THE candle flutters and darkles: —
  There is no sound within;
The embers in ashes redden,
  One flame crawls spectral and thin.

The candle flutters and darkles: —
  Wide and black is the door! I start
The Wind was the ghost that entered,
  And shook me and chilled my heart.

OTHER POEMS.

CLIO IN THE CAPITOL.

SEEN AT SUNSET FROM THE LIBRARY WINDOW OPPOSITE.

[Franzoni's Clock, with the marble sculpture of the Muse of History, Clio, listening and writing, upon a winged chariot, — one wheel of which, supported by the hemisphere of a globe, is the clock-face, — stands over the northern entrance of the Old Hall of Representatives, now assigned for the statues and portraits of our great public men. Through the centre of this Old Hall is the passage from the Rotunda of the Capitol toward the New Hall.]

I.

HERE, looking down, I see her Grecian grace,
    With the still halo of the last, low ray,
Motionless, beautiful, in the Sacred Place,
    While the late jarring footstep floats away.

II.

Lo, on the wingéd chariot where she stands! —
  (Its hurrying wheel notes the quick hour's hushed flight,
The half-globe beneath it) — in her patient hands
  The open book, the pen applied to write!

III.

In the Old Hall the men are changed to ghosts
  Whom erst she marked — who marked her not, perchance —
And there below, for those long-vanished hosts,
  Show marble shape and pictured countenance.

IV.

Daily across yon floor, long since so loud
  With partial schemes and strifes of public breath,
To the New Hall new-jostling statesmen crowd
  Through that White Congress of undying death.

V.

Men of the Past! your word her pages show —
  She heard, she saw, she knew you there, indeed!
O ye New-Comers, eddying to and fro,
  Behold the still Recorder and take heed!

VI.

There she remains, with listening face, and pen
Ready to give the patriot's deathless dower:
See!—living, speaking, acting, passing men!—
The Eternal Present on her flying Hour!

WASHINGTON, D. C., 1872.

TO THE MONTH OF MARCH.

[WRITTEN ON MY BIRTHDAY.]

MY life's first light thine own did bring,
    (Have I not shown myself thy child?)
Month of the bluebird, nurse of Spring —
    Fierce, stormy, gay, capricious, mild!

When thou didst come and bear me, lo!
    The lion came in, untamed and strong;
My earliest footprint was in snow;[1]
    Cold winds sung my first nursery song.

[1] Allusion to the observance of some little household superstition.

The lion, come in, goes out the lamb;

So may I, Mother, when life is past,

In green Spring pastures, sweet and calm,

With thy soft going, go at last.

A TRAGEDY OF LONG BRIDGE.[1]

ACROSS Long Bridge a woman with her child
Hurries — what backward glances quick and wild!

Dark is her face with Nature's mask of woe;
She is a slave — yes, this was long ago!

Behind her lay Virginia in the sun:
Before her shone the dome of Washington.

---

[1] Near the Virginia end of Long Bridge, at Washington, was once a slave-pen, and many years ago, it is said, a tragedy, somewhat similar to that related here, took place upon the bridge.

Behind her Slavery burdened day and dream:
Before her Freedom held a far, faint gleam.

Behind her, like a bloodhound in her track,
Came her fierce master, strong to drag her back.

Behind, before her — if she dreamed or saw
I know not — lo, the bond-securing Law! [1]

Panting she passes now the central tide,
Where the deep river shines on either side.

Hark! clamorous men behind her follow fleet —
Faster she flies with wild and piteous feet!

[1] The Fugitive Slave Law.

Look!—who approach her from the Northern
    shore?
She pauses, turns; she looks behind, before!

"Stop her!"— the servants of the Law behind:—
All must obey, though Pity speak "Be blind!"

She stands, all tremulous, helpless, looking round.
They close about her — she will soon be bound!

Hard arms are stretched — she springs with one
    shrill scream,
Her child close-prest, and sinks into the stream!

Baffled her master stands with raging breath —
Law cannot reach the Slave's Deliverer, Death!

. . . . Yes, it was long ago; but still at night
Across Long Bridge is seen the piteous flight.

Still, sometimes — who has seen I do not know —
Is seen the dreadful chase of long ago.

Fierce shouts are heard : lo! shapes of shadow
    run ! —
A dusky woman's, with her babe, is one!

Hark! a last shriek — the shrill appeal to Death!
The water laps the pier with marshy breath.

TO A LONELY WOODLAND SPRING.

PURE dweller in the shadows green,
  Glad hermit of the solitude,
Whose lovely work is wrought unseen
  Forever in the pathless wood!

Like thine I wish my task might be:—
  With the shy fountain's lonely birth
In Nature's close society,
  But sending beauty through the earth.

Such is the poet's life: a stream
  From his heart rising ever steals,
Wreathing bare use with beauty's gleam
  A rainbow on the busy wheels!

HOME-LONGING.

I LONG for thee, O native Western Land!
   I long for thy full rivers, moving slow
In their old dream, that changes not, but takes
The ever-changing vision of the air;
I long for these, the kinsmen of my youth,
And thy vast woodlands, murmuring weirdly still
Lost Indian legends, and thy prairies where
The bison's thunder, sinking far and vague,
Grows loud and near, and is the hurrying train.

WASHINGTON, D. C.

A VOICE IN OHIO.[1]

DECEMBER 17, 1877.

BY my quick firelight rapt and still,
   High on this black Ohio hill,
I think of him who crossed to-day
The snow-roofed boundary of our way
(His book upon my table lies,
Look from my wall his grave, sweet eyes),
The poet, who, in many a song,
Quickening unnumbered hearts so long,
Has breathed New England's spirit forth
From East to West, through South and North —

---

[1] Read at the "Atlantic Dinner" in Boston in honor of the seventieth anniversary of John G. Whittier's birthday.

Not the witch-burning bigot's rage,
That soiled her first heroic page,
But that, sweet, tender, warm and good,
Confirming human brotherhood;
Religious with diviner scope;
Wide-armed with charity and hope;
Lighter of household fires that bless
The fast-withdrawing wilderness
(Keeping old home-stars burning clear
In Memory's holy atmosphere);
Sowing the waste with seeds of light;
Righteous with wrath at wrongful might:
Such is thy better spirit, known
Wherever Whittier's songs have flown; —
Thy greater, larger, nobler air,
New England, thus is everywhere!

What though no kith or kin of mine
Came with the Mayflower o'er the brine,
(I know not — the dear Lord only knows:
No wide-branched family record shows!)
Grudge me not local pride — aye much —
In him, New England! French and Dutch
(We also fled for conscience' sake,
From zealot sword, revival stake),
Was I not taught by thy wise rule
In the great Western Yankee school?
Was I not shaped by thine and thee
In almost all that now makes me?
So, while my pulses warm and stir,
I truly am a New Englander!

Blessings be with him — praise, less worth;
Why ask long-added hours of earth?

Grateful, if given, these shall come.
Birds, sing to the reaper going home,
Singing himself — his work well-done.
Shine on him, slow, soft-setting sun!

NORTH BEND, OHIO.

BREVIA.

I.

A CERTAIN CONSERVATIVE.

HE holds a chrysalis aloft, infirm,
    Forgetting wings have borne away the worm.

II.

THE WHITE LIAR.

Beautiful, bright deceiver!
    On your lips are numberless lies,
But the truths they slay so lightly
    Live, above, in their heaven, your eyes!

III.

A STATUE OF JUPITER, BY PHIDIAS.

(Version from the Greek Anthology.)

Either Jove came to earth from heaven to show
    His very self to thee,
Or, Phidias, thou from earth to heaven didst go,
    The god himself to see.

IV.

NEW LIFE.

The Night — it passes, like a burdening dream;
    Quickened, I walk along a happy shore,
While low despairs, like mist along the stream,
    Climb, wondering at the sun, and are no more.

V.

AFTER-WEALTH.

Diamonds in tropic river-beds, they say,
Are found when the fierce floods are drained away;
So, in our lives, where passion-torrents flow
No more, shine wisdom's precious-stones below.

VI.

A FLOWER IN A BOOK.

The withered flower shall raise
A ghost of vanished days:—
From crumbled leaves a rose,
All fragrant-souled, shall rise
Within the heart and eyes

Of one who, dreaming, knows
The dust that was a rose!

VII.

A MOTH.

Poor moth, that fluttering through my candle-flame,
    Die of your sudden passion for the light,
From the great outer gulf of night you came,
    Then pass into utter night!

VIII.

INFLUENCE OF BOOKS.

Within the book-world rests the noiseless lever
That moves the noisy throngéd world forever.

IX.

WITH A GIFT.

Accept, I beg, this little shining stone,
Not for its worth — a friend's good-will alone.
Worn on your breast, I pray that it may show
Long where that friend rests safe and warm below.

X.

HOLY WORD.

God has unrolled His Bible in thy heart; —
To all the Holy Word of God impart.

THE DEAD STAR.

Yonder, in empty dark,
    Wanders, somewhere, a wasted sun,
    whose light,
Erst breathed abroad with life-creating spark,
Made hanging gardens of the circling night.

    Through Time's dark emptiness,
Some soul, that genius lit, goes, withered, wan,
Its flame to blackness fallen, purposeless —
    The dead star wanders with the fire-spent man.

ODE:

FOR THE OPENING OF THE CINCINNATI MUSIC HALL.[1]

MAY FESTIVAL, 1878.

I.

FOR ministries benign,
Complete, behold the gracious temple stands,
Whose stately walls full, fortune-sowing hands,
(Praise for the gift to the large-giving heart!)
Have builded in our eager Western mart,
    Denying Traffic's greed and Mammon's shrine.

[1] The gift of certain leading citizens to the city.

II.

To what civic Good or Grace
Shall we dedicate the Place?
—To Art and Industry, in friendly strife
Brightening and blessing life:

To smiling Toil, electric-fingered Skill
(Aladdin's light bidding by the huge bondman
    done,
    Dream-sandaled, tireless, still):
To quick Invention's prompt device,
With mechanism airy-nice,
    That, like the old fireside sprite,
Makes the wan maiden's task-work playful-brief,
    Letting her sleep by night:
To all that lathe and loom produce:

To Flora's garland, Ceres' sheaf,

And every fruit of soil and sun

(With the blithe vineyard's temperate juice)

To Sculpture's breathless-breathing charm,

And Painting's mirror soft and warm:

To each fair muse and every household grace:

To Use and Beauty bound in one —

    We dedicate the Place!

But, first, to her, the Muse of Music, her

Whose speech all spirits in earth and heaven

    know

(The native tongue of each far-sundered nation),

The loftiest, lowliest human minister,

    Exalting pleasure, soothing woe,

With heart, and voice, and organ's vast elation,

    To her shall be its consecration.

III.

From the wide doors of their rapt dwelling-places
(Whence ever-newly come their songs below,
    And whither, hence, they go),
Look, what high guests attend our happy rite,
With earth-woven wreaths but sphere-enchanted
    faces,—
    The Masters of Delight!
    —First he, of the elder days,
    Whom the great organ owns
With its vast-bosomed, earth-shaking, heaven-
    reaching tones,
(Let the proud servant throb his loftiest praise!)
Next he, who built the mighty symphonies,
One for each muse, who, chanting joy and
    peace,

Thrills us with awe and yearning infinite,
Picturing divine repose, love's world-embracing
    height!
    Then he, whose noblest strain
Brings Orpheus back to quicken earth again,
To conquer darkness, and the dread under-powers,
Charming lost love from the deep doors of Hell.
And lo, the choral master, highest in fame
(A thousand voices lift to greet him well),
Who breathes sure faith through these frail
    hearts of ours!
    And many another well-beloved name,
    Aye, many another, comes with these,
    Star-like, with spheral harmonies:—
        Welcome, each and all,
        To our festal Hall;
    Long be its music-lifted dome
For their abiding souls the transient home.

IV.

Hark! as if the morning-stars were singing
O'er the first glad Six Days' Task divine —
What rapturous sounds are these
Of quickening ecstacies!
Earth from her dark spell-bound slumber breaking,
To the sun's far-journeyed kiss awaking,
Lo, the blissful palpitation
Of the newly-warmed creation!
With a myriad mingling voices
All the electric air rejoices;
All about, beneath, above,
Rings the tender note of love;
Everywhere, around are heard
Fountain-laughter, song of bird,
Insect-murmur, wild-bee's hum,

Bleat of flock, and low of kine;—
Airs of new-born Eden bringing,
With her lilting, light-heart lay,
Dancing, singing,
May is come!—
Open doors and let in May!
Let Nature's full delight
Join with our banded joy, and crown our gracious rite!

v.

To this fair civic Hall,
Year after year,
New multitudes in many another May
Shall throng, repeating the bright festival
We celebrate to-day,

With happy rites to peace and culture dear;
Nor absent be our city's Patron then,
  In spirit, nor absent now —
  Commending loftier-lowlier ways,
The still, clear plainness of heroic days:
He after whom the founders, putting by
Swords wherewith late their sacred rights were
  won
(Associates they and friends of Washington),
And, building here in the fierce wilderness,
  Beneath the Indian sky,
The home we love and ask of Heaven to bless,
Called it for him, the soldier-citizen,
  The Roman at his plow!

THE POET'S BIRD.

"MANY a little song there flutters
   From my breast on sunlit wings:
In the world's wide sky it singeth —
   From my heart its echo sings."

Far away it flieth, singing
   Through the Mays of many Springs
(He was laid in lost Decembers):—
   From all hearts its echo sings!